History on your Doorstep

Volume 4

Five stories of Dublin history

by Dublin City Council's Historians in Residence James Curry, Cormac Moore, Mary Muldowney and Catherine Scuffil and Historian-in-Residence for Children Dervilia Roche

Edited by Cormac Moore and Mary Muldowney

Dublin City Council 2021
Decade of Commemorations Publications Series

First Published 2021
By Dublin City Council
c/o Dublin City Libraries
138-144 Pearse Street
Dublin 2

www.dublincity.ie

 Comhairle Cathrach
Bhaile Átha Cliath
Dublin City Council

©Dublin City Council

Designed by Anglo Printers Ltd.
Printed by Anglo Printers Ltd.

ISBN 978-1-8384635-2-6

All rights reserved. No part of this publication may be reproduced, stored in, or introduced into a retrieval system, or transmitted in any form or by any means (electronic, mechanical, photocopying, recording or otherwise, without the prior written permission of the copyright owner.

Table of Contents

5   Foreword, Lord Mayor of Dublin Alison Gilliland

6   About the Authors

9   Patrick O'Connell: Footballer and Football Manager
    JAMES CURRY, Historian in Residence, Dublin North West

17 A History of the Incorporated Hospital of Ireland
    CORMAC MOORE, Historian in Residence, Dublin North Central

29 Revisiting the Fallen: A tour of some war memorials in Dublin
    MARY MULDOWNEY, Historian in Residence, Dublin Central area

45 "What was there before the buildings?" A year with Dublin's young historians
    DERVILIA ROCHE, Historian-in-Residence for Children at Richmond Barracks

57 Why #Weaving in the Liberties?
    CATHERINE SCUFFIL, Historian in Residence, Dublin South City

Réamhra / Foreword

This fourth volume in the very popular History on your Doorstep series returns to the approach taken in the first two books, in which the Historians in Residence contributed short pieces about the history, locations and people they had encountered in their work in the different areas administered by Dublin City Council. This year they are joined by the Historian-in-Residence for Children.

The five chapters in this volume focus on different aspects of the city's history but they are united by the determination of the authors to continue catering for the enthusiasm and engagement of so many Dubliners with the story of the city's evolution, especially in the context of the revolutionary years that shaped Ireland. The response to the innovative role of Historian in Residence for Children demonstrates that this interest can commence at an early age.

The five chapters cover such diverse topics as the colourful life and career of football player and manager extraordinaire, Patrick O'Connell; the history of the Incorporated Orthopaedic Hospital of Ireland; a look at some of the war memorials in the city and how they reflect changing attitudes to national and international conflict; and the history of the weaving industry, once so important to Dublin and now the subject of vital work by local people in Dublin to restore the artistry and skills involved. The chapter by the Children's Historian in Residence covers her first year in the post and what she has learned from her young associates.

ALISON GILLILAND
Lord Mayor of Dublin

History on your Doorstep, Volume 4 is produced by Dublin City Libraries and is published by Dublin City Council as part of its Decade of Commemorations programme with the support of the Department of Tourism, Culture, Arts, Gaeltacht, Sport and Media.

About the Authors

JAMES CURRY received his PhD in History & Digital Humanities from NUI Galway in 2017, having previously graduated with BA and MPhil history degrees from Trinity College Dublin. He is the creator of a "History of Dublin" channel on YouTube and has published widely on twentieth century Irish history, including a book about Dublin radical cartoonist Ernest Kavanagh. James is a former committee member of the Irish Labour History Society and is the Historian in Residence for the North West area of Dublin City.

CORMAC MOORE has a PhD in History from De Montfort University in Leicester and an MA in Modern Irish History from UCD. He is Historian in Residence for Dublin North Central and is author of Birth of the Border: The Impact of Partition in Ireland, The Irish Soccer Split, and The GAA V Douglas Hyde: The Removal of Ireland's First President as GAA Patron.

MARY MULDOWNEY holds a PhD in History from Trinity College Dublin and a postgraduate qualification in Adult Continuing Education and Training from the National University of Ireland at Maynooth. She is the Historian in Residence for the Dublin Central area. Mary is the author of books and journal articles, often based on oral history interviews and she has a particular interest in labour and women's history. She is a member of the Grangegorman Histories Working Group and the organising committee of the Irish Labour History Society and she was a founding member of the Oral History Network of Ireland. She is a frequent consultant on other history projects.

DERVILIA ROCHE has been working in heritage and public history for over fifteen years. She has a BA in History of Art and Architecture and Music from Trinity College Dublin, and an MSc in Tourism Management from Dublin Institute of Technology. She has undertaken and published research on how children engage with heritage sites, and has worked across the city in education roles at historic sites and museums. She was appointed as Dublin's first Historian-in-Residence for Children, as part of Dublin City Council Culture Company's Creative Residency programme. The Historian-in-Residence for Children Residency @ Richmond Barracks is a partnership with Dublin City Council Culture Company and Dublin City Libraries.

CATHERINE (CATHY) SCUFFIL, MA, BBS HONS Dublin born and reared, Cathy's interest in local history was formed at an early age encouraged by parents who also shared a love of Dublin. She was honorary secretary/founder member of the Dolphin's Barn Historical Society (1986) compiling and editing their publication *By the Sign of the Dolphin* (1993) In addition to an honours Business and Management degree, Cathy also holds both a Certificate and a Masters in Local History from NUI Maynooth. Her master's thesis research was published by Four Courts Press as *The South Circular Road Dublin on the Eve of the First World War* and an abridged version awarded the silver medal by the Old Dublin Society (2018). Cathy was actively involved in a wide range of community events during the 1916 Rising centenary commemorations, researching the Rialto/Kilmainham 1916 Commemoration photographic exhibition and publication 1916 in the South Dublin Union for St. James's Hospital. Cathy is currently working as Historian in Residence with Dublin City Council for the South Central and South East Areas and is consultant historian for other projects.

The Historians in Residence project is part of Dublin City Council's work under the Decade of Commemorations (1912-22) designation and strives to break down barriers to history. The project is managed by Dublin City Libraries.

Contact them at commemorations@dublincity.ie
Twitter and Facebook @DubHistorians
www.dublincity.ie/residential/arts-and-events/decade-commemorations

Patrick O'Connell: Footballer and Football Manager

James Curry, Historian in Residence, Dublin North West

At 87 Fitzroy Avenue in Drumcondra there is a Dublin City Council plaque commemorating local footballer and football manager Patrick O'Connell. In the shadow of Croke Park, this plaque was unveiled on 5 June 2015 by Mike O'Connell, the subject's grandson, and Dublin Central T.D. Maureen O'Sullivan. Also in attendance at the ceremony were members of the Patrick O'Connell Memorial Fund who proposed the plaque, and retired footballers Steve Archibald, Bertie Auld, John Clark and Martin Buchan.

Dublin City Council plaque commemorating Patrick O'Connell, unveiled at 87 Fitzroy Avenue in Drumcondra on 5 June 2015
(Photograph by Paddy Cahill)

During his professional football career, Patrick O'Connell – who usually played in the defensive position of half-back and was 5 feet 11 inches in height – had the distinction of captaining both the Irish senior football team and Manchester United. After retirement, he emigrated to Spain and won a dozen trophies of varying stature as a manager, most notably the La Liga championship with Betis Balompié [Real Betis] in 1935. He also coached FC Barcelona during a pivotal period in their history, helping to save the Catalonian club from bankruptcy during the Spanish Civil War. This essay will provide an overview of his remarkable life.

Depiction of Patrick O'Connell playing for Belfast Celtic in a mural off the Falls Road celebrating his footballing career. This mural was unveiled in August 2015 and is the work of Belfast artist Danny Devenney

Patrick Joseph O'Connell was born on 8 March 1887 at the family home of 16 Mabel Street, located off the Clonliffe Road. His father, who was born in Kilkenny and also named Patrick, worked as a miller. His mother, Elizabeth (née Fox), originally came from Meath. She gave birth to twelve children, ten of whom survived. By 1899 the O'Connell family was living at 11 Jones's Terrace in Drumcondra, with the 1901 census recording nine children resident in the house, including the fourteen-year-old Patrick, who had already left school and was working as a glass fitter. He later secured employment at Boland's Flour Mill in Ringsend, where his father also worked.

A talented footballer, during his youth Patrick O'Connell played for the Dublin clubs of Frankfort, Liffey Wanderers (with whom he won the Empire Cup in 1904, 1905 and 1906) and Strandhill Juniors (with whom he won the Leinster Junior Cup in 1908). After turning twenty-one years of age, he then embarked on a career as a professional footballer by signing for Belfast Celtic, a leading Catholic-leaning team in the Irish Football League. O'Connell moved to Belfast in August 1908, a few months after his marriage in Dublin to Ellen Treston, the daughter of a carpenter who lived in North Strand. By the time of his marriage, O'Connell was working as a store clerk foreman, like his father, and living at 72 Fitzroy Avenue. He and his wife had two sons and two daughters together, with the first child, Patrick, born in Belfast shortly after their marriage.

The following year, in August 1909, O'Connell made the move across the Irish Sea and signed for Sheffield Wednesday, where he was playing when he won the first of his six international caps for Ireland. Living in a small house close to Wednesday's sports ground and occasionally supplementing his earnings by working at a local factory, O'Connell spent a few seasons operating on the fringes of the First Division club, making only twenty-one appearances in total, before dropping down to the Second Division to join Hull City in May 1912 for a fee of £350.

The Dubliner experienced more success competing for "The Tigers" than he had for "The Owls", earning a reputation as a "sound and judicious" defender. While representing Hull City, he played in all three of Ireland's International Association Championship matches during the 1913-14 season, when the team upset the odds by winning the annual tournament outright for the first time in the history of the now defunct competition, which had commenced three decades earlier. The Irish team previously shared victory with England and Scotland in 1903, but otherwise had a very poor championship record.

On 19 January 1914, Ireland defeated Wales away from home 2-1 in a match played at Wrexham. The following month, on 14 February, England were then despatched of with ease in a game played at Middlesbrough's Ayresome Park, with Ireland running out 3-0 winners as O'Connell captained the side. This meant that avoiding defeat in their final match would win the tournament for Ireland, and on 14 March, before a record crowd at Belfast's Windsor Park, a 1-1 draw against Scotland ensured that they clinched the championship. During the final match, which was played in miserable conditions, O'Connell suffered a serious arm injury but carried on competing to ensure that Ireland were not reduced to nine men at a time when no substitutions were allowed (the goalkeeper, Fred McKee was also injured and had to be replaced by an outfield player, Bill McConnell). Winning this tournament was a prestigious achievement for the Irish senior football team, who were unable to defend their championship for five years due to its suspension during the First World War.

So much did O'Connell impress during his appearances for Hull City and Ireland that he was signed by Manchester United in May 1914 for a near record sum of £1,000, a fee so large that it had to be paid off in instalments. He was soon made captain, the first Irishman to receive this honour, although the war limited O'Connell to making just thirty-five appearances for the club, and during the period he worked as a foreman in a munitions factory and competed for the likes of Rochdale Town, Clapton Orient and Chesterfield United due to relaxed wartime registration rules. In April 1915, O'Connell was implicated in a match-fixing scandal between Manchester United and Liverpool, although he escaped any ban or suspension for a notorious match in which he missed a penalty by a wide margin.

In August 1919, shortly after making his final appearance for the Irish national team, O'Connell moved to Scotland and signed for Dumbarton FC, where he had an uneventful spell, although he gained some coaching experience. He then returned to England after one season to sign for Ashington FC, living in the same Northumberland mining town where Bobby and Jack Charlton would later be born. In 1921, O'Connell became Ashington's player-manager, although he left the following year to embark on a coaching career in Spain, abandoning his wife and their four young children (Patrick, Nancy, Ellen, and Daniel) in Manchester.

From 1922 to 1929, O'Connell coached the team of Real Racing Club de Santander, situated on the north coast of Spain, west of Bilbao, and as well as winning seven successive Federación Cántabra trophies, oversaw the club's invitation to become one of the ten founding members of the Spanish First Division (La Liga). He then dropped down a division to coach Oviedo for two seasons, before moving south to Seville in 1932 to take over the reins at Betis Balompié (Real Betis), whom he led to their one and only Spanish league title during the 1934/35 season, an achievement which helped him to fulfil his long-held ambition of managing FC Barcelona, a club which had a history of appointing coaches with experience of British football.

In Spain, O'Connell committed bigamy in 1934 when he married a young Irishwoman named Ellen ('Ellie') O'Callaghan, who was unaware of his other family in England. When telling his London-based brother Larry about the second marriage, Patrick O'Connell was pragmatic and had the following to say:

> "I have met Ellie and she is Irish, and she lives here in Spain, working as a nanny. There cannot be above a dozen or twenty Irish women in this country and I have met one of them and we are to marry. This is a somewhat unconventional approach however, all that is past, is past. It was a different life, in a different country and what is past is finished.

Front cover of Sue O'Connell's 2016 book *The Man Who Saved FC Barcelona*, written with the intention "that Patrick O'Connell be rescued from oblivion". The author is the wife of the subject's grandson Mike O'Connell.

Ellen, the Ellen of then, was part of the passions of youth. She and I were ill-matched, we two touched briefly, intertwined, and separated. We will never meet again in this life. My children were cared for as much as was possible, given the distance and my resources. I did my best ..."

As a football manager, O'Connell developed a reputation for placing his trust in youth, liked his teams to transition as quickly as possible from defence to attack, and was friendly with his players although he demanded that they be as fit as possible. He was innovative in Spain, through focusing a lot on defending and making his teams difficult to beat. This was key to his greatest managerial success: when the unfancied Betis won the La Liga championship in 1935, they only conceded nineteen goals, fifteen less than the second-placed Madrid CF [Real Madrid]. Basking in his "moment of joy and triumph", O'Connell wrote to his brother Larry in London, "We've done it! The great FC Real Betis Balompié de Sevilla (Betis to its friends) has won La Liga. What more can a manager want than to take his team to the very top. Every man of them deserved it. It was a great moment of triumph. A singular event. Raise your glass to us. Betis is top of La Liga of Spain". During his first season as manager of Betis, O'Connell had led the club to promotion to the First Division after they finished mid-table the previous year.

O'Connell was excited about the FC Barcelona job, believing that the players at his disposal were talented enough to win the league championship within two years. However, things did not work out as planned for reasons that had nothing to do with football. During his time in charge of Barcelona, the team reached the final of the Spanish Cup in 1936, losing 2-1 to rivals Madrid CF (Real Madrid), and won the Mediterranean League the following year in a competition organised for clubs in the Republican area of Spain due to La Liga getting suspended with the outbreak of the Civil War.

Clay bust of Patrick O'Connell by the Dublin artist Joe Moran. The bronze version of this sculpture was donated to Real Betis before their home game against Real Sociedad on 3 March 2018 and is now displayed at the museum of the Spanish football club's Benito Villamarín Stadium.
(Photograph by James Curry)

The Spanish Civil War jeopardised FC Barcelona's existence. The club's President, Josep Sunyol, was assassinated; their sports ground was damaged during a bombing attack; and O'Connell and his players had to agree to take a sizable pay cut. With the club's future uncertain and danger abounding, the Dubliner – rather than resigning and leaving Spain – agreed to take Barcelona on a tour of Cuba, Mexico, and New York in 1937 as "Ambassadors of the Republic and of the Catalans". The funds raised during this four-month trip helped the club to avoid bankruptcy and rebuild in the aftermath of the Spanish Civil War. O'Connell was proud of the Americas tour he had led, feeling that it was essential for "the ordinary working man" in Catalonia to have their football club survive so that they could continue to lose themselves in escapism. "The great FC Barcelona will fight another day", he wrote to his brother Larry after returning to Europe, in a story that exemplifies the notion of the Catalonian institution being more than just a football club.

After his second spell in charge of Betis a few years later, O'Connell – who had the nickname of "Don Patricio" in Spain – began coaching their local rivals Sevilla in 1942, before returning to Santander later that decade and leading them from the third to the second division. By the early 1950s, O'Connell was looked upon as an outdated coach and began working as a footballing scout for little pay. In 1955, he and his wife Ellie made the difficult decision to leave Spain for London. O'Connell was sad to say goodbye to Seville, a city he loved and expected to live in for the remainder of his days. At the time of his departure for England, O'Connell told his brother Larry of the pride he felt at having "made no little mark on the world of football here in Spain", believing that the Spanish game "would not be where it is today without my contribution".

If not for the Spanish Civil War and Second World War, O'Connell would undoubtedly have achieved more as a football manager. Similarly, as a football player, the First

World War prevented him from reaching his full potential. Yet, despite all the obstacles, the Dubliner still achieved a lot in football and made history by captaining his country and Manchester United, before coaching Betis to their one and only La Liga championship and going on to help save FC Barcelona from financial ruin.

The final chapter in Patrick O'Connell's life was tinged with sadness. After separating from his second wife when she finally discovered the truth about his previous marriage and family, he spent his final years destitute, living in his brother's attic and claiming national assistance. The Dubliner passed away at St. Pancras Hospital in London from pneumonia on 27 February 1959, aged seventy-one, and was buried in a pauper's grave at St. Mary's Catholic Cemetery the following week.

Due to the efforts of the Patrick O'Connell Memorial Fund in recent years, he now has a gravestone which states that the former footballer and football manager is "remembered by many in Ireland, England and Spain".

Photograph taken during the formal opening of a Patrick O'Connell exhibition at Pearse Street Library on 1 December 2017 (Courtesy of Dublin City Libraries)
As well as the Dublin City Council plaque in Drumcondra, Patrick O'Connell is commemorated with an Ulster History Circle plaque in Belfast near the site of his former home on Albert Street. There is also a bronze bust of the Dubliner displayed in the museum at Real Betis's Benito Villamarín Stadium, donated to the Spanish football club in March 2017 and made by the East Wall artist Joe Moran.

Photograph taken during the formal opening of a Patrick O'Connell exhibition at Pearse Street Library on 1 December 2017.
(Courtesy of Dublin City Libraries)

Further Reading

- O'Connell, Sue. *The Man Who Saved FC Barcelona. The Remarkable Life of Patrick O'Connell.* Amberley Publishing, 2016

- Peake, Robin. *Patrick O'Connell, an Irishman Abroad,* in *Day, D. (ed.), Sporting Lives.* Manchester Metropolitan University, 2011, pp 55-72

- Shanahan, Jim. *O'Connell, Patrick Joseph ("Con"). Dictionary of Irish Biography.* https://www.dib.ie/search?search_name=o%27connell%2C+patrick

A History of the Incorporated Orthopaedic Hospital of Ireland

Cormac Moore, Historian in Residence, Dublin North Central

The inspiration behind the founding of the Incorporated Orthopaedic Hospital of Ireland was Dr Robert Lafayette Swan. Swan was born on 27 April 1843 in Durrow in Queen's County, present day County Laois. Robert's father was appointed to the Ballyragget medical dispensary in Kilkenny soon after Robert's birth. Robert spent most of his boyhood in Ballyragget. He went to medical school in Dr Steeven's Hospital in Dublin and at the age of twenty to the Royal College of Surgeons. Swan became resident surgeon of Dr Steeven's in 1867. He was also appointed assistant surgeon to the Royal Irish Constabulary and surgeon to the Great Southern and Western Railway company. In 1873 he was appointed lecturer in descriptive anatomy in the Steeven's School and he was elected president of the Royal College of Surgeons from 1898 to 1900. Swan also published many papers on orthopaedic topics in medical journals.

Dr. Steeven's Hospital (Courtesy of Dublin City Library & Archive)

Dr Swan was deeply moved by the plight of the poor, particularly in Dublin, and recognised that many of the city's poorest residents had bone problems which remained untreated for life. The streets included children who could never even hope to earn their own living as they suffered from a catalogue of conditions such as club feet, spinal disease, hip disease, rickets, unset fractures, and diseased stumps.

This imbued in him an interest in orthopaedic surgery and a desire to do something meaningful to help the poor children of Dublin. He recognised that orthopaedic treatment required not only special study but also special facilities. A general hospital could not provide the special long-term care required. With the aid of some friends, he opened a small hospital with six beds in his house in Usher's Island on the Quays in 1876. This was the start of what would become the Incorporated Orthopaedic Hospital of Ireland.

To survive, let alone thrive, funding from private donors was badly needed. From its inception in 1876, the hospital had an almost constant battle with funding to allow it to remain opened.

Edward Cecil Guinness, later Lord Iveagh, was one of the first to come to the hospital's aid, donating £50 when the hospital opened. His famous brewing family continued to support the hospital financially throughout much of its history.

Once established, the reputation of the hospital started to spread around the country, on account of its excellent work and the permanency of its results. Within seven years, the annual report of 1882/83 showed that eighty-two in-patients were treated that year and the bed numbers had risen from six to thirty. The young patients had an average residence at the hospital of eighty-one days. The average residence at general hospitals was eleven days at the time. The out-patient dispensary dealt with 5,840 cases that year. Of the eighty-two cases admitted, most of the children suffered from Club Feet, Spinal Diseases and Genu Valgum, otherwise known as 'Knock Knee'. No deaths were recorded.

Most of the patients came from Dublin, fifty-two out of the eighty-two patients, with the rest scattered throughout the country. In 1883, the hospital was almost reliant on funding from donors. It received £26 from G. R. Goodbody and £20 from John Jameson with many others contributing smaller amounts. It also received grants of over £100 from the Council of the Dublin Hospital Sunday Fund and £100 from Dublin Corporation. Both bodies continued to provide grants on an annual basis, which proved vital for the hospital's survival. Members of the public also supplied many gifts including papers, cards, books, clothing, dolls, toys, flowers, scrap books, illustrated papers, oranges, photographs, boots, flannel jackets, sheets, sweets, dressing gowns, turkeys, cakes, Christmas cards, large bracks, strawberries, and bags of apples. The Ladies Committee of the hospital organised 'Sewing Bees', making all the house linen and clothing required for the patients. Other benefactors provided drives and pleasant gatherings for the patients into the country during the summer months.

The Board of Governors contemplated closing the hospital, but with the help of donors and subscribers, it was able to move instead to a larger premises on Great Brunswick Street (present day Pearse Street) in 1883 which allowed the hospital to expand to thirty-five beds. The building served as the British Army's main recruiting office from 1910. To supplement its income, the hospital organised many events to secure funding such as balls, bazaars, amateur theatre occasions and sporting events.

Having moved to Great Brunswick Street, the hospital was able to help more children. Such was its reputation, there still was an ever-growing waiting list of children looking for help. In its sixteenth annual report from 1891/92, the hospital commented on the 'benevolent work' it carried out so that many helpless 'children would be rescued from a life of suffering, and rendered physically fit to become self-supporting, and thus the burden of taxation is lessened'. It also claimed 'the remarkably low death rate of the institution' is 'due to the skilful surgical staff'. Out of 1,155 cases from 1876 to 1892, only seventeen deaths were recorded within its walls since its foundation.

Despite the constant struggle for funding, the hospital and its ancillary services continued to expand. The bed numbers increased to forty. The dispensary dealt with more and more out-patients year after year. On top of his surgical work on site, and regularly donating his own money to the hospital, Dr Robert Lafayette Swan opened his country house, 'Delaford' in Templeogue to convalescing patients, providing the advantage of clean country air as opposed to the city's smog-laden air where 'delicate patients' could be sent. Six beds were made available at 'Delaford'. In case of an epidemic, patients could be moved there too. A hot-water system was introduced to the hospital in 1895, the same year a gymnasium was added. The gymnasium was particularly important when splints or plasters were removed, and the children had to be taught to walk and the muscles exercised. A gym instructor was employed on a full-time basis. The gym was opened to the public at a moderate charge, which was used to offset the expenses of its maintenance.

The orthopaedic hospital again looked to relocate to expand its services. A plot of land adjoining Great Brunswick Street on Tara Street became available, but despite the hospital's efforts to secure the plot, it was acquired by Dublin Corporation compulsorily as a site for a Fire Brigade Station. It finally secured a new site in 1902, a spacious and suitable mansion at 22 Upper Merrion Street. With its move to Merrion Street, the hospital took on the name 'The Incorporated Orthopaedic Hospital of Ireland'. The move increased the bed numbers to fifty-six.

The relocation entailed great expense with the need to remodel the sanitary arrangements to suit hospital needs; the building of a registrar's office; a new gymnasium fitted with mechanical instruments, apparatus, and appliances; and a

Orthopaedic Hospital in Merrion Street

complete operating theatre, sterilising room, and anaesthetic room. The expense was somewhat alleviated by a grant of £1,500 from Lord Iveagh but it was still burdened with a bank debt of £1,872. The gym facilities continued to expand, and a qualified medical gymnast and masseuse was hired, who conducted daily classes in which each pupil was personally instructed and treated. The gym was refitted with modern Swedish apparatus.

In the annual report of 1908, it was stated that there was a 'need to let the public

Gym at Orthopaedic Hospital in Merrion Street

know more about the help they give' to the poor of Ireland 'as they are totally reliant on the generosity of benefactors. They had no endowment nor Government grant. The hospital was £2,000 in debt. The report continued:

> *The average length of residence in this Hospital for a patient is one hundred and twenty seven days, whilst that for General Hospitals is eleven days. The Orthopaedic is the only Hospital in Ireland that specialises in treating congenital disabilities, 'and to be effective in its work must keep the patients under treatment for a long period'. Patients also need apparatus, splints, surgical boots, etc. 'The Nursing Staff require special training to carry out the treatment' of disabilities 'by manipulation'.*

The annual report of 1908 claimed that patients were treated from thirty-one of the thirty-two counties of Ireland. Patients would also come from further afield, some coming from Southport and Liverpool in England, one even came from the Isle of Man. In 1908, the hospital also opened a ward under a veranda in the garden, an open-air ward to place children suffering from tubercular bone-disease, with the open air very beneficial to them. There were sixteen beds in the ward. The hospital claimed it was the first open-air ward in Ireland and possibly even the first in the United Kingdom or Europe.

Open-air ward which opened under a veranda in the garden of the Orthopaedic Hospital in 1908

By 1911, there were seventy-one beds occupied in the hospital and six at the convalescent house at 'Delaford'. With most children remaining in the hospital for lengthy periods, the Board of Governors decided to provide education to those children. In its 1911 report, the hospital stated 'To deal effectually' with Orthopaedic cases:

> *Prolonged residence in Hospital is necessary. In many cases children are under treatment for a year or more. As this occurs during the school period of the children's lives, it has been felt for some time that something should be done to provide instruction for the patients. Application was, therefore, made to the Board of National Education, and, with the help of Mr. Justice Ross (Sir John Ross, the Lord Chancellor of Ireland), who is a member of that Board, and who has long been a kind friend to the Hospital, a Teacher was appointed exclusively for the Hospital, whose salary is paid by the Board of Education. Instruction is being given daily to fifty-four of the patients in National School subjects, including singing and breathing exercises. The children thoroughly enjoy the teaching. Sewing is also taught to the girls.*

Younger children were taught on the Kindergarten system. A hospital representative later remarked that 'not only has the school proved successful in improving the mental and moral tone of the children, but it is believed to have been of great benefit to them physically. The interest the little ones take in the classes has brightened their lives, improved their health, and consequently made easier their treatment'. It was also commented that 'It is hardly realised that some of these children have never been to school at all owing to the difficulty of getting them to school, especially in the country. But once in this Hospital the school comes to them, bringing them a new source of pleasure and interest besides aiding them to become wage-earners in the future'. A "School Dental Clinic" was provided soon afterwards too, 'so that the children's teeth may be preserved and cared for during their stay in hospital'.

In 1912, a mortuary was built, but at a location sufficiently isolated from the hospital. A year later, a quarantine ward was opened to prevent the introduction of infectious diseases; a new bathroom was installed in the admission room and wash-hand basins with hot and cold water were provided for each ward at considerable expense. A complete X-Ray installation was also acquired, seen as a valuable asset to the treatment of orthopaedic cases.

The crippling costs of running the expanded hospital were further exacerbated by the start of the First World War in 1914. The annual report of 1917 recorded that:

> *Contracts for food are now impossible to obtain, and the difficulties of catering for such a large family are enormous. Every possible economy is practised, but children must be given the necessary nourishment and workers cannot be too severely rationed. The increased expenditure is also due to the fact that all hospital and household requisites are very expensive, often costing more than double the pre-war price.*

There was also a large increase in the price of coal and coke. By 1919, the hospital had a debt of £543. The war also resulted in the death of one of the governors, Lieutenant W.S. Drury, who was killed while serving in France on 29 January 1916. That same year, in November, the founder of the hospital, Dr Swan also died. According to the governors, 'that to the late Surgeon Swan must be given the credit not only of originating the Hospital, but also of bringing it to its present state of development'. The hospital was also affected by the War of Independence and subsequent civil war, stating that 'owing to the disturbed state of the country there has been a considerable reduction in the subscriptions and donations'. There still was a huge demand for its services, with one observer claiming that for every patient availing of the hospital facilities there were fifty more that ought to be there. According to Theo Mortimer, who wrote an article on the hospital's history for the Dublin Historical Record and who was himself a patient there:

> *The hospital was poor, very largely, if not altogether, because the work it did was largely unknown to the philanthropic public. Its worth, its virtues, its mission, was all concealed behind high brick walls and what was then considered a forbidding name. The doctors received no money for their*

> services, but the hospital had to be maintained, beds had to be provided, food and clothing purchased, and the cost of all this was greater than the income... It existed entirely from voluntary subscriptions.

In the early 1920s, rachitis or rickets predominated both on the wards and at the dispensary. The 1923 annual report recorded that '"Rickets" is a disease which appears in very early childhood, but its effects continue all through life, and are often most disabling. Special orthopaedic treatment was essential to correct or minimise the many affects. The majority of patients required apparatus such as splints, plaster jackets and surgical boots. Of the 194 cases of children hospitalised in 1923, sixty-three cases were related to rickets. The installation of an artificial sunlight lamp in the gym helped in improving results in cases of rickets and other types of ailments.

In 1926, the hospital celebrated fifty years in existence where it had treated over 30,000 children in that time. In most cases very young children were cured of club-foot and rickets by manipulation and plaster appliance. That same year, the distinguished British orthopaedic surgeon Sir Robert Jones, on a visit to the hospital, advocated a "Country Home" in connection with the Hospital. He believed that children's orthopaedic hospitals should be in the country 'where the patients suffering from rickets and tuberculous bone disease would have the inestimable advantage of sunshine and fresh air'.

The 'open-air' ward of sixteen beds was wholly insufficient for the demand, with the hospital claiming 150 'open-air' beds were needed. An open-air home or hospital in the country was required and the hospital therefore began a fund to secure such a building. Donations to the Open-Air Extension Fund advanced slowly with just £1,154 collected by 1930. Between £10,000 and £12,000 was needed before a start could even be made to acquire such a hospital.

On top of many incidents of club feet and rickets, a large number of children were admitted for infantile paralysis or polio to the orthopaedic hospital. The 1933 annual report stated 'Paralysed children who are unable to walk, and, indeed, barely able to crawl, are often admitted to the Hospital, and, after a course of surgical treatment and gymnastic exercises, are eventually taught to walk, and return home able to lead a more normal life and do useful work. Children such as these would never have been able to do more than crawl about had they not received treatment in a Hospital such as this'.

Despite the slow rate of donations, the hospital was able to declare in the 1940 annual report a positive development in its quest for a new home, stating:

> For many years past the Governors of this Hospital have had continually before them the hope of obtaining a fresh air home for the children and the necessity of securing new premises in view of the termination of the lease of

A History of the Incorporated Orthopaedic Hospital of Ireland

Upper Merrion Street. With regard to the first, an effort was made to unite with the Children's Hospital, Harcourt Street, but this did not materialise. Since the last Annual Meeting the Governors have purchased Blackheath, Clontarf, with about six and a half acres, the former residence of the late Mrs. Gibson Black, who, it is of interest to record, was a Life Governor of this Hospital. In securing this House and ground the two ideals are within view of being attained, for an "Open-Air" Ward has been built which will accommodate some fifty beds while the building itself will hold approximately seventy beds, and it is hoped in time to extend the open-air wards. The wards are large, lofty, well-lit, and very sunny, with a southern aspect, and it is hoped to have the Hospital ready for occupancy by June at latest.

The Governors have had to sell their War Stock and to obtain a loan from the Bank, for the purchase and reconstruction of the premises. The loan has now been exhausted and will require about £8,000 more money to equip the place thoroughly and pay the balance due to the Contractors...Money is needed to equip the operating theatre, Plaster Room, X-Ray Department, Gymnasium, Electric equipment, etc.

A year later the hospital reported that:

Orthopaedic Hospital at its new site of Blackheath in Clontarf

'The new Hospital has given added accommodation – from seventy-six to one hundred and thirteen beds to date – greatly increased space, and the advantages of country surroundings. Sunshine and fresh air have undoubtedly hastened the cure of the children in the Hospital, and the general improvement in the little patients is evident. Part of the grounds has been put under cultivation, and a certain amount of fresh vegetables has been already obtained'.

The Irish Times reported in June 1941 that the move from Merrion Street to Clontarf just took one day. The article stated:

'The highly complex problem of moving a whole hospital, with staff and patients numbering one hundred and fifty persons, as well as all equipment and furniture, was achieved in one day without a single hitch in Dublin, yesterday, when the sixty-five-year-old Orthopaedic Hospital of Ireland was transferred from 22 Upper Merrion Street to its new home at "Blackheath", Castle Avenue, Clontarf, in sixteen ambulances and fourteen lorries'.

One hundred and twenty members of the local security forces, the Irish Red Cross and many friends and helpers assisted in making the move a success.

The new home, with considerably more space, allowed the hospital to be enlarged at different junctures from 1941. With more children being admitted, three full-time teachers were appointed to the school in 1946. The out-patient dispensary in Merrion Street remained, with an X-Ray department being equipped there. A Nurses' Home which consisted of twenty-eight bedrooms for sisters and nurses, a matron's flat, a sister's sitting room and a nurse's sitting room was opened in 1952, costing £29,250. A year later, a new physiotherapy exercise room and twenty-four new beds were added to the hospital.

The hospital was facilitated in meeting the costs of its new home and the various expansions by government support and the continued aid from donations from the public. Religious bodies such as the Catholic Church also helped. In 1944 the Catholic Archbishop of Dublin Dr John Charles McQuaid visited the hospital and donated £750 towards improvements to the open-air wards.

By the 1960s, advances in medical science saw the role of the hospital change considerably. From its foundation, the hospital dealt with patients from birth to about sixteen years of age. With children being diagnosed at birth, there was no longer a need for lengthy stays in the hospital. Children could be treated immediately, without any need to be hospitalised in many cases. The success of immunisation against polio in babies also lessened the need for hospitalisation. Being mindful of the grave shortage of beds for adults in the city's general hospitals, the board of governors offered forty beds for use by adult patients. The first adult patient arrived on 4 April 1972.

At the time of its one hundredth anniversary, a new out-patient clinic building was completed. The President of Ireland Cearbhaill Ó Dálaigh attended the centenary celebrations. In the 1990s, plans were put in place to move the wards from the main house to a state-of-the-art hospital facility. The new hospital building was completed in 2009.

The hospital now consists of five wards with a total compliment of 160 beds where it continues to provide orthopaedic rehabilitation treatment as well as providing an 80-bed Active Rehabilitation Unit for older people.

Thanks to Michelle Fanning, Chief Executive Officer of Clontarf Hospital, for her assistance in researching this article.

Further Reading

- Clontarf Hospital Annual Reports

- Mortimer, Theo. *"The Incorporated Orthopaedic Hospital of Ireland." Dublin Historical Record, vol. 60, no. 2.* Old Dublin Society, 2007, pp. 161–66

Revisiting the Fallen: A tour of some war memorials in Dublin Central

Mary Muldowney, Historian in Residence, Dublin Central

In November 2018, when we were commemorating the 100th anniversary of the ending of the First World War we were also thinking of the forthcoming centenaries of other conflicts that were fought much closer to home. The focus and function of remembrance in Ireland has evolved over the last century, most recognisably in relation to conflict. Between 1914 and 1923 the country was divided by wars, nationally and internationally, and during the subsequent one hundred years there has been change in how those who were casualties of the First World War, the Anglo-Irish War of Independence and the Civil War were commemorated. In recent years this has been largely due to the recognition that the Peace Process in Northern Ireland and the ending of political violence would benefit from overcoming the barriers created by the differences in remembering that were evident between Northern and Southern Ireland.

In this chapter I am going to look at some examples of how Dublin City commemorated war dead in the twentieth century, focussing only on physical embodiments of remembrance. I intended to present these as a self-guided walking tour, but my favourite sites are not necessarily close to each other, so I am concentrating instead on monuments that are within walking distance of the city centre. Space precludes an exploration of the drama, literature, poetry, song, and visual art that are often linked to memorialisation.

Attitudes have changed over the decades and to an extent that shift has been reflected in the built memorials that were created to honour those who lost their lives. In 1918 in particular and since then, there has been a significant difference in the perspectives expressed by the memorials in the two States in Ireland. The main one, of course, has been the focus on remembrance, with monuments in the south reflecting contrasting perspectives. One viewpoint marked victory over Britain in the struggle for independence and in the decades following the Civil War, but it could also raise uncomfortable memories of the birth of the Free State and the political differences that shadowed its development. The other point of view, more problematic in the aftermath of the revolutionary years, focussed on those who had lost their lives in the

Great War and was often seen as an uncomfortable reminder of British rule. For Ulster unionists, their service in the First World War represented a great sacrifice on behalf of Britain, earning them the right to opt out of Irish self-government. For nationalists, participation in the war was largely seen as a mistake and following independence in 1922 it was superseded in popular memory by the struggle for self-determination. In the one hundred years since the war ended, support for commemoration has ebbed and flowed, mainly according to which part of Ireland it was taking place in. The fact that more Irish nationalists than unionists died fighting in the British Army during the Great War does not change the enormity of the losses a century ago, regardless of the prism through which they are viewed, but the impulse towards a more unified public commemoration, however motivated, should not be at the expense of distorting public understanding of the actual history. Some commemorative practices, on both sides of the border, led to crude stereotyping, in an effort to find meaning in past traumatic experiences.

The Volunteer (Courtesy of Dublin City Library & Archive)

It is evident that the words 'monument' and 'memorial' have been used interchangeably in remembrance of war dead in Ireland and there is not necessarily a matching chronology to when statues were created and installed in the streets of Dublin. According to art historian Paul Gough a monument is 'a structure, edifice or erection intended to commemorate a person, action or event.' In contrast, definitions of 'memorial' focus on the preservation of specific memory and on their iconographic role in evoking remembrance. A monument usually has scale, permanence, longevity, and visibility. Memorials, by contrast, are often more intimate, local, and personal, though they are usually durable and open to public view in some manner. The monument has often been built to promote specific ideals while the memorial is essentially a retrospective form, idealising a past event, historic figure, or place.

The Irish Volunteer Monument at Blacquiere Bridge in Phibsborough illustrates this point. The statue commemorates members of the 1st Battalion of 'C' Company of the Dublin Brigade of the Irish Volunteers who fought and died during the Easter Rising (1916) and the War of Independence (1919-21). It was not unveiled until 19 February 1939. While the base of the statue shows scenes from Celtic mythology, its style is very reminiscent of similar monuments to soldiers who fought in the First World War, mainly to be found in Northern Ireland. Leo Broe (1899-1966) was the sculptor and he had been a member of the Irish Volunteers.

The initial remembrance of the First World War was conducted while Ireland was still at war, undivided and part of the United Kingdom. Information about losses began to filter through as early as 1914, when most of the nationalist population was still firmly pro-Home Rule. Word about the casualties initially galvanised recruitment, especially as the forum for commemoration at that time was mainly notices and stories in the country's newspapers. Dublin's Evening Herald favoured adding photographs to their reports. The practice of naming the dead was extended in the immediate aftermath of the war into the creation of multiple plaques and memorials that listed the casualties from specific institutions, such as churches and workplaces. Staff from railway companies were frequent targets of recruitment in the early years of the war, usually with the promise of their jobs being kept open for them on their return. On the south wall of the concourse at Heuston Station there are two plaques, illustrating the different traditions of commemoration.

One plaque lists staff members from the Great Southern and Western Railway who were killed in the First World War and the other commemorates Sean Heuston, outlining his service on the railway and his role in the 1916 Rising, before his execution in Kilmainham Gaol. Heuston is also remembered in a statue in the Phoenix Park, sculpted by Laurence Campbell (1911-1964) and unveiled in 1943. It can be seen in the People's Garden in the Phoenix Park.

Memorial plaques at Heuston Station (Courtesy of irishwarmemorials.ie)

Sean Heuston statue in the Phoenix Park (Wikipedia Commons)

One of the less well-known sites of remembrance in Dublin is the Grangegorman Military Cemetery on Blackhorse Avenue. The cemetery was opened in 1876 to serve as a graveyard for the soldiers of what was then Marlborough Barracks (now McKee Barracks) and their families. Since the British Army did not repatriate soldiers killed overseas until recently it contains the remains of soldiers from across the British Empire who died naturally or were killed in action in Ireland. After 1923, only service men and their next of kin could be buried there and some of the headstones commemorate the soldiers' wives.

Two graves in the Grangegorman Military Cemetery (Photographs by Mary Muldowney)

The cemetery is currently managed by the Office of Public Works to the standards set by the Commonwealth War Graves Commission and is the largest military cemetery in Ireland. It is a calm and peaceful site that is also evocative of the sadness and waste of war. First World War casualties are interred throughout the graveyard, as are others who survived the war but died later. There is a row of grave markers of soldiers who were killed on 10 October 1918, when the M.V. Leinster was torpedoed and sunk as it left Dublin, with many soldiers on board.

The graves of those who were killed between 24 April and the first week of May in 1916 include some of the 118 soldiers who were killed in the course of the Easter Rising. There are numerous graves of Sherwood Foresters and South Staffordshires who suffered serious casualties when they attempted to cross Mount Street Bridge on the Grand Canal. The last major conflict in the twenty-six counties involving the British Army was the War of Independence and the cemetery holds the graves of

Graves of victims of the sinking of the M.V. Leinster
(Photograph by Mary Muldowney)

soldiers killed between 1919 and 1921. The last burial took place in the cemetery in 1999.

An equally peaceful site lies within a short walk from Blackhorse Avenue. This is the very well-known Arbour Hill Cemetery, where fourteen of the sixteen executed leaders of the 1916 Rising are buried. The cemetery was originally a British Army site until it reached capacity in the 1870s and Grangegorman replaced it. Following the burial in a mass grave within Arbour Hill prison, the 1916 leaders were first memorialised in the 1920s, when Harry Clarke was commissioned to create a stained glass window in the church next door. This church was renamed the Church of the Sacred Heart in 1927 and is still operative as the church of the Defence Forces.

In 1955 the prison walls were moved to separate the yard where the mass grave was situated and the 1916 plot was created in the space. There are two stone plaques on the surrounding wall; one which features the text of the Proclamation of the Republic in English and Irish and the other is carved with the names of sixty-two men who died in the course of the Easter Rising. There were many commemorative events in the cemetery in 2016, for the centenary of the Rising.

In 1919, a parade was held in Dublin as part of the United Kingdom-wide celebrations of 'Peace Day' on 19 July, while the early engagements in the War of Independence show that there was already a fractured approach to remembering the Fallen, as the Irish Republican Army used the dead of 1916 to inspire their members and supporters. These issues were further complicated by the struggle for independence and the increasing divide between nationalists and unionists. There was still much enthusiasm for remembering the dead of the World War, but at the same time, there

Part of the text of the Proclamation of the Republic in Arbour Hill Cemetery, 1965
(Courtesy of Dublin City Library & Archive)

was an eagerness to commemorate the casualties of the War of Independence. In the Irish Free state there was a gradual and deliberate 'forgetting' of the war and the Irishmen who had died in the uniform of the British Army, as historian F.X. Martin pointed out in the course of the fiftieth anniversary ceremonies in 1966.

The policy of 'forgetting' became an official one as the new regime became more entrenched, even before Fianna Fáil took over. British war service was seen as irrelevant and was even said to be traitorous. Those who died for Ireland in the 1916-1921 period were considered to be far superior to those who had died fighting for the British Empire. The fact that many Catholic Irishmen thought they were fighting for Ireland rather than the British Empire when they enlisted in 1914 and believed in the promise of Home Rule was ignored.

War Memorial Gardens in Islandbridge, 1939
(Courtesy of Dublin City Library & Archive)

By the 1930s, numbers were decreasing at the Armistice Day ceremonies but there was still an annual long march from the city centre in Dublin to the memorial garden at Islandbridge. The idea of a national memorial had originated as early as 1919 and a committee was set up to raise funds, headed by Sir John French, then Lord Lieutenant of Ireland. The committee raised £50,000 in public collections. While various locations and settings for a permanent war memorial were suggested and rejected over the next decade, the Memorial Committee set about commissioning an interim project. This was to be a set of books, the pages of which listed the names of every Irish soldier who had been lost in the war. The books were compiled, designed, and produced during one of Ireland's most turbulent periods - during the War of Independence and the following Civil War - before being published finally in 1923. The books listed just under 50,000 names, occupying 3,200 pages over eight volumes altogether. The books are housed in the specially designed Book Rooms in the Garden.

In the meantime, then President of the Executive Council, W.T. Cosgrave offered the Islandbridge site, which was substantial in size at 150 acres. It was then known as Long Meadows and consisted mainly of allotments. The distance from the city centre was no accident and meant that when Éamon de Valera took over, he could live with the Memorial, despite criticism by some republicans that the state should not play a role in the plans.

Sir Edwin Lutyens was commissioned in 1930 to provide a design for the site and it was laid out in the period from 1933 to 1938, under the supervision of the Board of Works. These gardens are now one of the most famous memorial gardens in Europe. A special construction crew was hired to build the monument and lay out the buildings and the gardens, half of them veterans of the British Army and the other half veterans of the

Free State Army. They used only manual tools so that the numbers of men employed on the scheme could be as great as possible. When war broke out in 1939, the official dedication of the Memorial was cancelled, and it was forty-six years later before it actually took place. Taoiseach John Bruton officially opened the completely restored park and memorial, which is now maintained by the Office of Public Works. It was not until 2006 that the Irish state held an official commemoration there for the Irish dead of the First World War, when President Mary McAleese and Taoiseach Bertie Ahern marked the 90th anniversary of the Battle of the Somme on 1 July.

One of the four Book Rooms in the War Memorial Gardens
(Photograph by Mary Muldowney)

Wreaths laid at War Memorial Gardens for Armistice Day, 11 November 2018
(Photograph by Mary Muldowney)

One of the most beautiful sites associated with commemoration is the Garden of Remembrance in Parnell Square, which is dedicated to the memory of all those who gave their lives in the cause of Irish Freedom. It was created for the fiftieth anniversary of the Easter Rising on the historic grounds next to the Rotunda Rink, where the Irish Volunteers was formed in 1913. The land was bought from the Rotunda Hospital in 1939 and a competition was launched for its design. The architect Daithí Hanly (1917-2003) won the commission for design of the garden, which was formally opened by Éamon de Valera in 1966. In 1971, a magnificent sculpture, 'The Children of Lir', by Oisín Kelly (1915-1981) was installed at the south end of the garden, in a space that Hanly had created especially for it, with a poem by Liam Mac Uistin (b. 1938) behind it. The sculpture was an interesting choice in managing to avoid military connotations, which might have been expected to be included in the context of a monument to dead combatants. The story of the Children of Lir and their nine hundred years of exile was intended by Oisín Kelly to reflect the long centuries of the Irish struggle for freedom and independence.

Children of Lir in the Garden of Remembrance
(Courtesy of Dublin City Library & Archive)

Death of Cuchulainn in the GPO
(Courtesy of the Royal Irish Academy, Modern Ireland in 100 Artworks)

One of the best-known sites of remembrance was not originally created to commemorate conflict and war and its unveiling in 1914 preceded many of the events mentioned in the previous descriptions.

Oliver Sheppard's famous statue of the Death of Cúchulainn is housed in the General Post Office in O'Connell Street, a building which is synonymous with memories of the 1916 Easter Rising and is in itself a monument to an almost unified interpretation of the history of the independent state. Its selection as a symbol of the struggle for an independent republic was largely because of Éamon de Valera's determination to take control of that legacy for the Fianna Fáil party that had come to power in 1932. The government was planning an elaborate nineteenth anniversary commemoration of the Rising and the Cúchulainn statue served as the centre piece. The sculptor was a friend of Pádraig Pearse and he taught Willie Pearse in the Dublin Metropolitan

Cross of Sacrifice, Glasnevin Cemetery (Wikipedia Commons)

School of Art. Historian Róisin Kennedy points to the unification of Celtic myth and Christianity in the framing of Cúchulainn as an evocation of the pietà, which was consistent with the inclusion of religious ceremonies in the inauguration of memorials to the dead.

In the twenty-first century a process of reconciling the disparate traditions of commemoration has come to a head and for the most part a new maturity has emerged in the official approach to remembering the people who died one hundred years ago, regardless of the uniform they were wearing. The unveiling of a Cross of Sacrifice to honour Irish soldiers who died in both World Wars took place at Glasnevin Cemetery, Dublin, on 31 July 2014. It was unveiled by President Michael D. Higgins, together

The Hauntings soldier in St. Stephen's Green, November 2018
(Photograph by Mary Muldowney)

with the President of the Commonwealth War Graves Commission, the Duke of Kent, who both laid wreaths. The ceremony coincided with the centenary of the outbreak of the First World War.

There are many monuments and memorials throughout the city that have not been included here, and indeed, most towns and villages in Ireland have sites of memory, the majority created or installed up to and including the fiftieth anniversary of the Easter Rising in 1966. One difference between ceremonies in that period and the more recent commemorations for the Decade of Centenaries has been the involvement of so-called 'ordinary people' in marking significant events in the evolution of the Irish state and the evidence that attitudes to that history have also evolved.

In November 2018, the 'Hauntings Soldier' was installed in St. Stephen's Green to mark the one hundredth anniversary of the Armistice. This was a statue created from scrap metal by Martin Galbavy and Chris Hannam, two Dorset-based blacksmiths. The statue depicted a world-weary soldier returning from the war and it attracted huge crowds from around the country to see it. Sadly, in its last week in Dublin it was vandalised with red paint. However, if the perpetrators thought this would be approved of, they were much mistaken. There was outrage from most commentators and thousands of people turned out on the last day of the Soldier's 'visit' to remember the casualties that he represented.

The Hauntings soldier in St. Stephen's Green, November 2018
(Photograph by Mary Muldowney)

Further Reading

- Bateson, Ray. *Memorials of the Easter Rising.* Irish Graves Publications, 2013

- Higgins, Roisín. *Transforming 1916: Meaning, Memory and the Fiftieth Anniversary of the Easter Rising.* Cork University Press, 2012

- Irish War Memorials. www.irishwarmemorials.ie

- Jeffery, Keith. *'Echoes of War'* in John Horne (Ed.), *Our War: Ireland and the Great War.* RTE/RIA 2012 edition, pp. 261-276

- Kennedy, Roisín. *'The Death of Cúchulainn in the GPO'* in *Atlas of the Irish Revolution.* Cork University Press, 2017, pp. 917-920

"What was there before the buildings?": A year with Dublin's young historians

Dervilia Roche, Historian-in-Residence for Children at Richmond Barracks

For the past year I've been working as the Historian-in-Residence for Children at Richmond Barracks, as part of Dublin City Council Culture Company's Creative Residency programme. The programme creates partnerships to try out ideas, test new approaches and add to the cultural story of the city.

The role of Historian-in-Residence for Children is the first of its kind in Dublin, and it aims to encourage the children of Dublin city to create lifelong connections to history. This residency is made in partnership with the Culture Company and Dublin City Libraries and complements the successful Historian-in-Residence programme run by Dublin City Council. My work in this role involves working with children aged nine to twelve across the city, both inside and outside of schools, through history workshops, projects, summer camps, and more. These activities aim to bring history to life for children, to help them uncover their own local and social history, and to further their curiosity and explorations of Dublin and history in general.

The role is based at Richmond Barracks, a building of historical importance located in Inchicore, which is home to a library, garden, cafe and Culture Connects, a programme of cultural activities that celebrate the experiences and interests of the local communities and people. Most of the activities and projects of the residency have so far taken place online, due to the Covid-19 pandemic, with a gradual move now towards a blended programme of activities for children which will be both online and in-person. Having now reached the end of my first year in the role, I can reflect on the many things I've learned from the children I've met, about their perceptions of history, their interactions with it, and the things we can do to encourage this interest as they grow.

Richmond Barracks. The Historian-in-Residence for Children role is based at Richmond Barracks, Dublin 8 (Photograph courtesy of Dublin City Council Culture Company)

It's all about stories

Understanding the past can empower children, as it can with adults too. It can contribute to our values, judgement, decision-making, and even our sense of identity. It helps us to see our place in time, and our place in the world, with the potential to help us to feel more connected to our local area, our city, and even the people in our lives. To many children around the city, history is already a passion, and we can work together on how to dig deeper on the topics they find interesting. For other children, it can be more about discovering the huge variety of types of history and inviting them to discover what they find most appealing.

Children are drawn to stories from a young age, and all they need is an ability to listen or read before they are capable of delving into the world of the past. From primary school age, children can begin to understand the importance of different types of historical sources, examining evidence, thinking critically, and asking questions about what they read and watch, skills that will undoubtedly stand to them in all aspects of their life. Indeed, learning about history is often about much more than just that, as local history in particular brings in many aspects of geography, while other activities may involve learning about art, languages, science, politics, and any number of other subjects.

The activities throughout the first year of this residency have reflected the variety of interests that children across the city have. Like all of the programmes run by the Culture Company, it began with having chats. I met with various families and school groups across the city and talked to the children about their interests in history, their favourite stories or eras from the past, how they usually find out about history, and what they know or like about the history of Dublin. Various themes emerged from this which allowed us to create activities that could be enjoyable and meaningful for the children who participated.

These activities have included long and short projects with school groups, public workshops at weekends and midterms, summer camps, and longer projects such as a monthly children's history book club. Aside from these interactions, I've also collaborated with children on video projects and developed self-guided resources for families. The variety is designed to give as much opportunity as possible for children to engage with history, allowing them to find something that suits their interest and learning style.

The kind of topics we have looked at in these activities have included things like Vikings, castles, the World Wars, the Easter Rising, art history, as well as the origins and traditions associated with different holidays throughout the year. School projects have included examining the local area using historical maps and other sources, as well as Christmas projects where the children became oral historians and

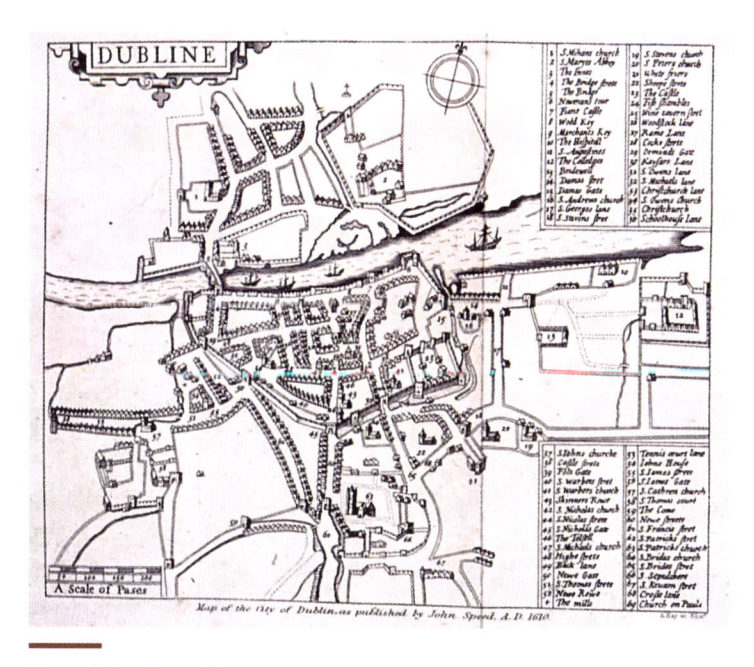

Map of the City of Dublin by John Speed, 1610. Children often enjoy visualising the city's past by using historical maps (Courtesy of Dublin City Library & Archive)

interviewed family members about their memories of that time of year. I've also collaborated with other historians, artists, and writers, to deliver workshops on history illustrating and writing, such as during the Children's Book Festival and the Dublin Festival of History.

The sessions are made as interactive as possible, even if taking place online, incorporating discussion, art and crafts, games, quizzes, scavenger hunts, and plenty of visual aids. This variety helps to keep things interesting for the children and also accounts for different learning styles. We also talk about the work of a historian and how the children can continue their own research in the area. As the residency progresses, I am always learning more from the children and gathering more feedback and ideas for what we can work on next.

Schools and book clubs

In terms of where children develop an interest in and awareness of history, children in the 9-12 age group learn history as part of SESE (Social, Environmental and Scientific Education) in primary school. A lot of children I spoke with were excited about particular history topics if they had just completed a school project on them or if their teacher was particularly focussed on local history and bringing them on walks and visits. However, more often than not, children have told me that their interest in a particular part of history comes from sources other than school.

Children's section of Coolock Library. Reading historical fiction is often a gateway to exploring history in-depth (Courtesy of Dublin City Libraries)

I spoke to many who told me that their interest in a particular historical era started when they read a book about it. It became clear that reading historical fiction was a brilliant gateway for many young people, placing them into a particular time and place in the past, which then led to them wanting to learn more about that time. Whether or not the story they read was strictly accurate was outweighed by the interest and enthusiasm it created in spurring them on to do their own research and further investigate the topic.

This was part of the reason behind setting up a children's history book club, where the children nominate novels or graphic novels relating to history for us to read and discuss. We explore the real historical context behind the setting of the story and relate it to Irish and Dublin history where possible. The books we've read have ranged in history from the World Wars and the Dublin Lockout right up to the recent and ongoing history of Syrian refugees. Having the anchor of the characters' experiences to talk about allows us to really explore sometimes complex ideas and events, as seen from some of the comments participants have made during those sessions. "It seems like revolutions are always to do with money", one remarked while we discussed a book set during the Russian Revolution, or "I liked that Betty was standing up for what is right" when discussing a book set during the 1913 Lockout. The book club members have gotten to know each other, despite some of them meeting only online so far, and this allows them to feel at ease and have an honest discussion. Discussing history with each other rather than just with myself or a teacher is something children often get a lot from and may be more likely to remember.

As well as books, television and online videos are huge sources of information for children, as might be expected. While they may be less likely to relate to Irish or Dublin history, we can usually still find some kind of link to the city, and it can be really enjoyable for children who live here to bring those worlds together. We can also reuse some of the ideas of these, such as the strong use of humour in many children's history television shows. Several children also spoke about history they had encountered through musicals and how this sparked their interests also.

Local histories and lots of questions

The children I spoke to were less likely to know much about local history. When they did know a little, it had often been from stories from family members, such as a funny, memorable story a grandparent had told them about a specific place local to them. This can really show the power of family interactions when it comes to learning about the past and the potential of things like interviewing older family members about memories, or even just having discussions within the family while visiting historic sites. Some children spoke to me about being shown old objects their grandparent owned and the conversation that was sparked by looking at these. For some, they wanted to begin by learning about the history of their own home, such as a participant in a video project we undertook, who commented "I would love to know who lived in our house in 1875".

When asked about their favourite time from history to learn about, many children appeared to have a huge interest in ancient civilisations. The Ancient Greeks, Romans and Egyptians were frequently mentioned in terms of their way of life back then and their influence on how the world is now. Sometimes this extended into talking about the Vikings of Dublin who are perhaps viewed in a similar way. Many children are particularly interested in the myths and belief systems of these civilisations, such as the stories of gods and goddesses. This can be used to discuss the importance of story-telling in many cultures and can be easily related to Ireland's storytelling history and folklore.

Stories and places with an element of mystery or spookiness are also often very appealing. One girl spoke to me about wanting to explore old cemeteries, jails, and hospitals. Separately, I was asked on a video project we undertook: "Old churches have scary things like skulls and gargoyles, but why is that?". Mysterious places like old castles and ruins can spark imagination as children begin to picture how it might have been in the past. Exploring places in general can bring history to life for children and create a really memorable experience. Children have told me about how excited they were to go inside places like castles, or how much they like to explore local historical gardens. Taking in the environment like this can often be the starting point for wanting to explore its history further.

Historical spaces that can be explored by children can be a starting point for learning about the past. Royal Hospital Kilmainham
(Photograph courtesy of Dublin City Library & Archive)

Drimnagh Castle. Children are often curious about the darker side of medieval life and history in general
(Photograph courtesy of Dublin City Library & Archive)

It has been really clear that many children are interested in the darker side of history. Topics like the Famine and the Holocaust are often brought up in conversation, usually accompanied by questions about how these events came to be. It shows a real curiosity and often maturity that they want to understand and acknowledge these parts of history. I'm often also asked about diseases and plagues from the past. These can sometimes stem from an interest in the gorier aspects of history, but of course can also reflect our current pandemic as the children draw comparisons between what they've read about and what they are currently experiencing. Being curious about gory and dark history is also seen in other subjects, such as medieval castles, as one question that was asked in a video project we undertook was "When you trespassed into Drimnagh Castle, did you actually get your head chopped off and stuck on a fence outside?"

Children often also mention the Titanic and are perhaps interested in the tragic nature of that too. Some are also fascinated by the way of life onboard the ship and the stark contrast of life above and below deck, showing the children's interest in understanding class divisions and inequality. The interest in class divisions is perhaps also seen in how many children enjoy learning about the royal families of the past, the grandeur of their lifestyles, and the connections between families found when exploring royal family trees.

I've talked to many children who have a real interest in military history. This has generally involved an interest in one or both of the World Wars, which again stemmed from some of the many historical fiction books set during those times. During history quizzes we have taken part in, the children sometimes come up with their own history quiz questions, and these often centre around the World Wars, with questions like "What did soldiers in the First World War use to get rid of lice?".

My workshops often make use of historical maps, and one thing that is often really appealing about these is discovering how much smaller Dublin used to be, and that many places they know as being built-up were once fields or wild areas. Some children have made remarks such as "It's crazy how small Dublin was in the seventeenth century" and asked, "What was there before the buildings?".

To many children, "history" means going as far back as we can. Lots of children are interested in the Stone Age people, their way of life and tools. But even more, children often talk about what was here before there were humans, asking me about dinosaurs, woolly mammoths, and other animals of the past, as well as how natural features like cliffs and mountains were formed. All of these things are seen as part of the same story of how things came to be as they are now.

Some topics mentioned by children are those which they have perhaps heard about but don't yet have a full understanding of, and the workshops provide a space to address these. Some of these topics would include questions about the 1916 Easter Rising, and the history of British rule in Ireland, wanting to properly understand how they came about and what they actually involved.

Of course, children, like adults, vary hugely in their interests and the particular part of history that they may want to learn more about can often reflect this, with their interests often based on their own hobbies. This might include things like a curiosity about the history of fashion, food, art, music, or sport. These are things that may not all be part of the school history curriculum but can be very relatable for children.

As the majority of my history activities have been online so far, due to pandemic restrictions, this has also been a learning experience. While online sessions can be challenging with children, particularly in terms of encouraging conversation and the inability to help children individually with activities, it also allows for us to interact in new ways. Online workshops can be good for sharing images very clearly so visual aids can be incorporated in the workshops. This might include things like maps and timelines for context, old photos of places, images of online records for them to decipher, and Google Street View images so the children can recognise the part of Dublin we're discussing. Online sessions can also include audio clips of oral histories. For some children, using the chat text box has allowed them to chat to myself and the others in a way that they may not have in person, and being based at home also means some children may be more comfortable and allows them to use materials with which they are familiar.

The more exploring the better

When encouraging children to explore history, there are a few key things we can do. One would be keeping the history as relevant as possible, by making links to the local area, or to stories, places and concepts the children are already familiar with. In a similar way, we can try to make it personal to the children to whom we are chatting. When history is retold, it is always by its nature biased to some extent so we can try to avoid this too by sharing stories and facts and allowing the children to make up their own minds, again encouraging them to question and critique things. Many children (and adults) struggle with remembering dates and names, but often we can tell the stories of history without involving too many of these. In many cases, children won't yet have a sense of the chronology of major historical periods so specific dates can sometimes feel a bit meaningless to them. It can be much more effective to focus on the events, stories, themes of history and why they may be important. In my work, I try to ensure that the history activities are not just educational, but fun too. If they work well, they will also encourage reflection, inspiring the children to think about their place in the stories, and to think about how the stories make them feel.

We can encourage children to read as they are likely to encounter historical stories from books. Becoming a library member will make it easy for children to access and try out different kinds of books. Remember that history comes in many shapes and sizes and does not need to always directly relate to what children are learning in school. It may be that you can relate something from their favourite television shows or online videos to a particular historic place or exhibition in Dublin. Museums and historic sites are becoming more and more accessible for children, with many special resources and activities available for different age groups so they can be a great way to explore a topic further.

Exploring local history with children can be much easier than it may first appear. Even something as simple as taking a walk in the local area and looking up at features on buildings can be really effective. Many library branches have a local history section where you can find more information. There are online resources like historical maps to compare the area now to how it was hundreds of years ago. There are also online maps of places like national monuments, excavation sites, and buildings of architectural significance, all of which can be used to piece together the story of the area. Online census records and other types of records can be used to investigate the stories of people who lived in the area, and children may particularly enjoy reading up on local folklore, much of which is also available online. Of course, talking to people about history can be hugely effective for children. Asking an older family member or neighbour about their memories can help children to understand their family or local history too in a way that may be very rewarding.

As we progress out of the pandemic and into the next era, it will be interesting to see the effect of the past two years on children's perception of history. Many adults have gained a greater awareness of their local area and local history during this time, and it may be that this was the case for children also. Many children also gained experience during school closures in self-directed learning and in using digital learning resources, all of which have the potential to make it easier for them to explore history and other subjects that interest them.

As I've learned from the past year, the children of Dublin have a huge interest in history, spanning across many subjects and topics. They have demonstrated an ability to show curiosity and understanding of sometimes very complex subjects, to be respectful of the past, but to always have fun at the same time. As we move forward into a post-pandemic world, we can be sure the future of the city will be safe in their hands.

About Creative Residencies

We create partnerships to try out ideas, test new approaches and add to the cultural story of the city.

Creative Residencies encourage makers and experts to pilot new partnerships with organisations. By bringing creative people and organisations together and by connecting through culture and conversations, we will develop and share new ways of working.

The Creative Residency programme is made by Dublin City Council Culture Company. The Historian-in-Residence for Children Creative Residency @ Richmond Barracks is a partnership with Dublin City Council Culture Company and Dublin City Libraries.

For further information about the Historian-in-Residence for Children programme and details of current projects, please visit **linktr.ee/DublinHiRC**

History on your Doorstep

Why #Weaving in The Liberties?

Catherine Scuffil, Historian in Residence, Dublin South City

The recent formation of The Liberties Weavers, a community group dedicated to bringing the tradition of handweaving back to the area, is the most recent development in the long history of weaving in The Liberties area of Dublin. In former days this inner-city district, sometimes called Dublin's oldest village - was at the heart of Ireland's textile production and there is much evidence of this once thriving industry still in existence in The Liberties area today.

With the ongoing regeneration programme and many new developments in The Liberties, a considerable number of archaeological investigations have taken place, each revealing traces of our past. The finds from these investigations have been varied, with many, particularly in the Newmarket and Thomas Street areas, directly relating to weaving. Some trace the industry to the Hiberno-Norse era, with finds such as stones that acted as loom weights, as well as various items of equipment like shears and spindles. One relevant and local placename that dates back to this era is 'The Glooey' – Thie Gloigee, Manx Gaelic for Weaver's Shed, and is still mentioned by locals in the Blackpitts area when referring to a small roadway linking Fumbally Lane, and Malpas Street located off lower Clanbrassil Street.

The skill of weaving on an industrial scale particularly in The Liberties area was greatly advanced with the passing of an Act of Parliament in 1662. This Act for encouraging Protestant strangers and others to inhabit and plant in the kingdom of Ireland was the beginning of a phased, mainly (continental) Huguenot, immigration into Ireland, and had the considerable support of the Viceroy of Ireland, James Butler, first duke of Ormonde. The intention behind this Act was to strengthen the numbers in the Protestant community whilst in tandem creating a vibrant and organised business community, particularly in Dublin city. The first group to arrive in this wave of immigration were mainly French and Flemish economic migrants. The second – and larger - group were mainly French Protestant refugees, fleeing the regime of King Louis XIV, which pressurised communities to convert to Catholicism. The third phase of immigration expanded the Protestant numbers in Ireland even further, attracting people who were mainly west of England Anglicans, with a range of different trades and skills, with some merchants in their numbers and others who had agricultural backgrounds.

Among these different groups were a considerable number of skilled weavers who immediately upon arrival, set about developing their trade primarily in The Liberties of Dublin. By 1674, the second Earl of Meath had developed a market within his Liberty – called Newmarket - to facilitate the trade in the raw materials of wool, hides and flax, as a support service to these growing industries. In the years that followed, this market and the areas nearby also facilitated trade in the finished woven cloth. In 1682 the Weavers' Guild, also known as The Guild of the Blessed Virgin Mary, had their own hall built on The Coombe. The siting of a market, together with the Guild Hall on The Coombe, resulted in the entire area becoming synonymous with all aspects of the weaving trade.

Initially weaving in The Liberties centred on the woollen trade, supported by nearby agricultural settlements in the outer suburbs of then rural Dublin. However, as early as 1699, in response to the effects of Irish wool production on England's related industry, the British parliament passed the Wool Act to prevent the production of Irish wool products, and more importantly, their export. This was essentially an effort to destroy the Irish woollen industry. As a consequence, the weavers in Dublin started exploring other means of developing their business by producing different outputs such as linen, cotton, silk and eventually the world-famous Dublin poplin, a textile woven with a warp of wool and a weft of silk meaning it could not be subjected to taxes and tariffs.

Local placenames dating from that time reflect the growth of this industry. The most obvious is Weaver's Square and its earlier incarnation of Cloth Square.

Weaver's Square (Courtesy of Dublin City Library & Archive)

Nearby open fields, which were traversed by watercourses and tributaries of the river Poddle, provided the perfect area to wash, bleach and dry woven cloth. To facilitate the drying process, large wooden frames were used to stretch out the wet cloth, with tenterhooks securing the material in place. This process resulted in yet another new local placename derived from the weaving process. The Tenterfields was soon shortened to The Tenter's, a name still assigned to this part of Dublin today.

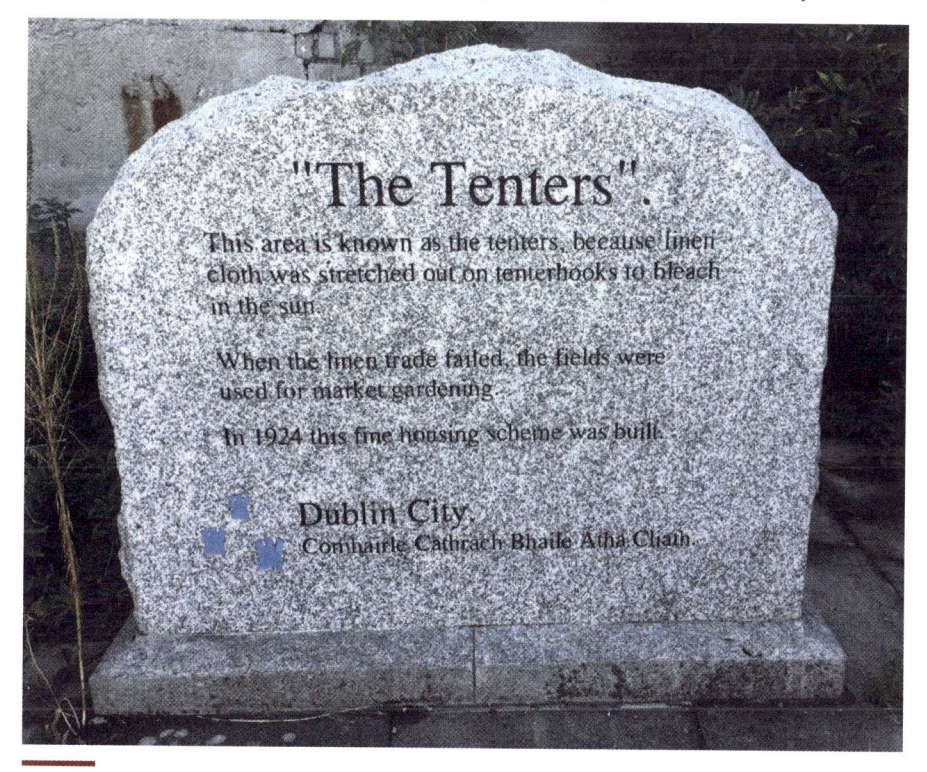

The Tenter's Stone (Courtesy of Maria O'Reilly)

A link street from Weaver's Square to Cork Street is called Ormond Street, as an acknowledgement to the duke. The French speaking weavers left placenames such as Marrowbone Lane from Maire le Bon Lane and a small laneway linking Weaver's Square to The Tenter's, today called Cow Parlour, which had been derived from the French phrase Coup D'ourlet, meaning the hemcutters.

The three alleys off Meath Street also reflect the weaving community, with Flag Alley, Crosstick Alley and Engine Alley all holding clues. Flag Alley was named for the manufacture there of flags and banners of the various trade guilds of Dublin; Crossticks Alley gave a nod to implements used in the weaving process and Engine Alley originally came from Indian Alley, reflecting the importation of silks and cotton from India. This became corrupted to the Dublinese 'Injun', later becoming Engine.

Cow Parlour (Courtesy of Dublin City Library & Archive)

Engine Alley (Courtesy of Dublin City Library & Archive)

As a result of another Act of Parliament passed in 1708, the old Dublin parish of St. Nicholas Without was divided, with part of it given a new denomination of St. Luke's. The new church for this parish was then erected on The Coombe. There have been suggestions that the church of St. Luke's was built primarily for the benefit of the conformist French Huguenot weavers who by this time populated the local area. However, there are relatively few French entries in St. Luke's parish registers. The Huguenots held their worship in the Lady Chapel in St. Patrick's Cathedral. Whilst the Huguenots may not have used St. Luke's in any great numbers, there was a considerable number of other weavers and those with links to the poplin, silk, cotton, and wool manufacture that did, and their names are much associated with this parish. With so many skilled workers and their families living in the neighbourhood, the parish of St. Luke's was one which benefited from permanent employment and huge wealth generation, certainly in the early years of its' existence.

By 1745 a new guildhall was needed for the expanding community of weavers and with the financial support of David Digges La Touche, a prominent member of the Huguenot community, this landmark building was eventually constructed on The Coombe.

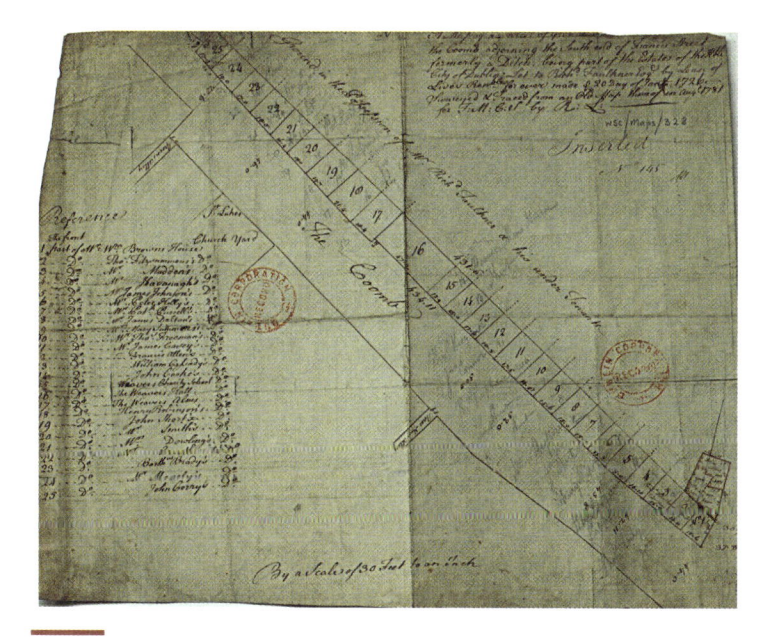

Plan of The Coombe (Courtesy of Dublin City Library & Archive)

A key feature of the new Guildhall was a statue of King George II set in an alcove above the main door. The king is holding symbols of weaving implements, such as a shuttle and a spindle.

THE WEAVERS' HALL, WITH STATUE OF GEORGE II.

The Weaver's Hall (Courtesy of Dublin City Library & Archive)

Other industries also grew in support of weaving. Carpenters to build the looms, bobbins, spindles and shuttles, dyers to colour the cloth, laundries to wash and dry the fabric, ring, and rope makers to support the sail and marquee weavers. Upholstery, silk, and lace for carriages were also included in this range of skills. They built a particular style of house within which to carry out their business. These famous gabled Dutch Billies were once a key feature in The Liberties.

The children and grandchildren of the early weavers later found their way into municipal, economic, religious, and political life and helped build our city. They were involved in building the Grand Canal, they were bankers – the La Touche Family being a good example. They became Lord Mayors, with at least two of them buried in family tombs or vaults in St. Luke's parish graveyard. One was the renowned master weaver Richard Atkinson, who also financed a widow's alms house for the parish in nearby New Street. His warehouse premises were located at Merchant's Arch at the Ha'penny Bridge on Dublin's quays.

The Act of Union of 1801, which created the United Kingdom of Great Britain and Ireland had a devastating effect on Irish manufacture and trade. The loss of fashionable society from Dublin to Westminster during sittings of the parliament in particular, effected the weaving industry which had all but collapsed as the national economy slumped. Many involved in the weaving industry were left destitute, a situation that worsened as the century progressed. The British Parliamentary papers of 1829 quite shockingly report the Earl of Kildare's statement to parliament that

WHY #WEAVING IN THE LIBERTIES?

Weaver's Houses (Courtesy of Dublin City Library & Archive)

Merchant's Arch, view from Temple Bar side (Courtesy of Dublin City Library & Archive)

'20,000 looms were silent' in Dublin. That loaded, short sentence tells us so much about this area at the time. In advertising its annual charity sermon, the parish of St. Luke's then described itself as "the poorest parish in Dublin".

In an effort to assist the by now impoverished Liberties Weavers, Thomas Pleasants financed the building of the Stove Tenter House in 1815 on land close to Weaver's Square. This was to assist the weavers when wet weather made the drying of cloth almost impossible, with the building providing an indoor area to stretch and dry cloth in rainy weather. Wood burning stoves or furnaces in the basement area provided heating to assist the drying and airing process.

The Liberties weavers kept re-inventing their industry by finding new ways around the problems as they arose. The creation of Dublin poplin, a fashion favourite in the mid 1800's, that even formed part of Queen Victoria's trousseau, was a fabric created to get around the trade tariffs imposed. But yet again, the success of Dublin poplin was disastrous for the English cotton and wool industries, resulting in more controls and tariffs being imposed. Specific controls meant that material could not be imported directly into Ireland but would need to be brought through England first. Consequently, the Dublin weaving trade, went into a slow and almost terminal decline. Around this time, the Stove Tenter House was closed, as there was no longer a need for the service. The building was later acquired by Fr. John Spratt, a Carmelite priest, who repurposed it as a night refuge for homeless people. In subsequent years it became part of the sisters of Mercy convent and schools on Cork Street.

Elements of the weaving tradition managed to survive the difficult times following the Great Famine of the 1840s but the slow decline of the industry due to industrialisation and cheaper imports added to the overall demise of the area. An examination of Thom's Almanack and Official Directory of 1862 for the Weaver's Square area shows a number of the properties on the square are now multi-occupancy tenements. However, two businesses associated with the weaving and textile industry were still in operation, namely James Becket who describes himself as a 'silk mercer' and the much larger premises of Richard Eustace's public woollen dying and manufacturer. Eustace's would later locate to even larger premises on nearby Cork Street.

By 1911 some 441 people living in the Usher's Quay and Merchant's Quay electoral divisions described themselves as 'weavers', some in silk, others in poplin and worsted, a type of hardwearing material usually used for labourer's clothing. Among the larger concerns still associated with the textile trade at this time were Frys of Cork Street, who specialised in poplin ties and other products. Nearly every woman of working age living in Ardee Street in the same census was employed as a tie maker. Whilst men were generally employed in the Ardee Brewery, Frys was the local factory employing women. Their advertisements tell us that they also made mufflers to wear in the new form of transport – the open automobile. Elliott's of Brown Street were also poplin weavers.

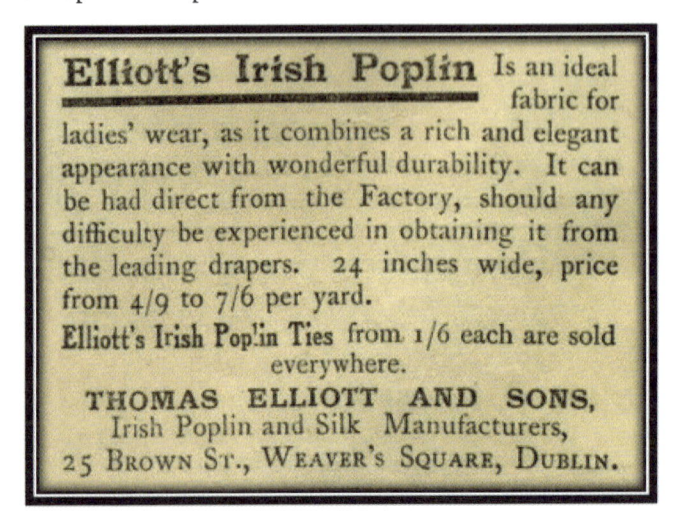

> **Elliott's Irish Poplin** Is an ideal fabric for ladies' wear, as it combines a rich and elegant appearance with wonderful durability. It can be had direct from the Factory, should any difficulty be experienced in obtaining it from the leading drapers. 24 inches wide, price from 4/9 to 7/6 per yard.
> Elliott's Irish Pop'in Ties from 1/6 each are sold everywhere.
> **THOMAS ELLIOTT AND SONS,**
> Irish Poplin and Silk Manufacturers,
> 25 BROWN ST., WEAVER'S SQUARE, DUBLIN.

Elliott's Advertisement in *Dublin Brigade Review,* **1939** (National Association of the Old IRA)

Why #Weaving in The Liberties?

The City Woollen Mills was located in Emerald Square just off Cork Street and Bailey and Gibson, the tent and marquee manufacturers, had their premises on the South Circular Road, just beside Dolphin's Barn village. The houses in Haroldville Avenue, Reuben Street and Avenue, together with those in Carrick Terrace were built in the early 1900s by Bailey and Gibson for some of their employees.

Considering the fact that a considerable number of people from The Liberties were employed in the various weaving industries, combined with the high numbers from the area involved in the Irish Revolution, it was not unexpected to find people from that trade directly involved in the cause. One such individual was Liberties born Michael Mallin.

Like many of his generation, he had served time in the British Army and when he returned to Dublin in 1902, he then became a silk weaver, apprenticed to his uncle James. To add to his credentials, he also became secretary to the weaver's trade union, under which capacity he set up the Silk Weaver's Hall (sometimes called the Cleaver Hall) in Donore Avenue off Dublin's Cork Street. When he joined the Irish Citizen Army, he was appointed Chief of Staff by James Connolly. During the 1913 Lockout, when he lost his own shop in Meath Street, he led a strike and negotiated on behalf of the silk workers at a factory in Hanbury Lane. During the 1916 Rising, he was Commandant-in-Charge of the St. Stephen's Green/College of Surgeons Garrison for which part he was executed in Kilmainham Gaol in May 1916.

Michael Mallin (Courtesy of Dublin City Library & Archive)

Nellie Bushell from Newmarket Street was also a local associated with the Irish Revolution who was a Liberties weaver.

Using her skills, she made kilts for Na Fianna, and in her evening work as box office clerk in the Abbey Theatre she carried messages for 'F' Company, 4th Battalion to which she was attached. During the

Nellie Bushell Advertisement in *Dublin Brigade Review*, 1939 (National Association of the Old IRA)

65

Josie McGowan (Courtesy of the McGowan family, via Micheál Ó Doibhlín)

Easter Rising, she carried dispatches between the garrisons at Jacob's Biscuit Factory and Marrowbone Lane Distillery and also assisted the garrison at Watkin's Brewery when they transferred to Marrowbone Lane. After the Rising she had to leave her home in The Liberties as it was regularly raided by Crown Forces. She relocated to Inchicore where she continued her revolutionary activities, including hiding arms for the rebels.

Another woman from the area involved in the Rising was Josie McGowan of Dolphin's Barn Street. She too was a weaver by trade. During the Easter Rising she served in Marrowbone Lane Distillery following which she was arrested and imprisoned in Kilmainham Gaol. Upon her release from prison, she assisted in the organisation of the National Aid and Volunteer Dependents Fund and in June 1918 was involved in Lá na mBan, an anti-conscription event organised by Cumann na mBan. In a protest meeting at Foster Place in September 1918 Josie was one of a number of people baton-charged by police during which she was fatally injured. She died on 29 September 1918; she was 20 years of age.

In the years that followed the revolution, with the emergence of the Irish Free State, the decline of the weaving industry continued. Many women from the area found work in sewing factories, which again was something of a tradition in this area throughout the 20th century. Many current residents fondly recall working in places such as Glen Abbey, Henry Whites and Blair Linens – to name but a few.

In recent years, the craft of weaving had all but died out in this community. There was only one weaving concern left operating, that being the Botany Weavers in Emerald Square near Dolphin's Barn. The premises they were working out of was located on the site of the old City Woollen Mills. However, other long-standing industries were also in decline; whiskey distilling was no longer happening in the area and Guinness was the only brewery left in recent times. The emergence of the old whiskey triangle with recent developments, together with the imaginative Weaver's Park, with its stylised loom entrance gate set the scene for the notion of bringing weaving back to The Liberties.

The Liberties Weavers evolved as a class of learners following four taster sessions run in early summer of 2019. This initiative under the Historian-in-Residence programme was fully supported by the Dublin City Council Community Development team in the South West Inner-City area, and with Marja Almquist, a master weaver of the Yarn School in Goldenbridge. The energy in the newly configured Timberyard Studio on a weekly basis was quite simply a joy to experience. The Liberties Weavers looked at the Liberties Village around them, considered the colours that defined the place, the #Colours of the Liberties. They recreated it using suitably coloured threads and a wide variety of themes, often with a basis in the rich history of the area. Their outputs telling the story of the weavers themselves and the history hiding in plain sight, were displayed in the newly built Hyatt Centric Hotel marking the beginning of the new, but old, tradition of #Weaving In the Liberties and enhancing the spirit of one of Dublin's oldest villages.

The Liberties Weavers (Courtesy of Weaving in the Liberties)

Further Reading

- Corrigan, Vawn. *Irish Tweed, History, Tradition, Fashion.* O'Brien Press, 2020

- Crawford, WH. *Domestic Industry in Ireland.* Gill and McMillan, 1972

- Crawford, WH. *The Handloom Weavers and the Ulster Linen Industry.* Ulster Historical Foundation, 1994

- Curtis, Joe., *Harold's Cross.* History Press Ireland, 2011

- Dunlevy, Mairead. *Dress in Ireland.* Holmes and Meier, 1989

- Dunlevy, Mairead. *Pomp and Poverty, a history of silk in Ireland.* Yale University Press, 2011

- Hoad, Judith. *This is Donegal Tweed.* Shoestring Publications, 1987

- Hughes, Brian. *16 Lives, Michael Mallin.* O'Brien Press, Dublin, 2012

- Johnston, Máirín. *Around the Banks of Pimlico.* O'Brien Promotions Dublin, 1985

- Mitchell, Lillias. *Irish Spinning, Dyeing and Weaving.* Dundalgan Press Dundalk, 1978

- Mitchell, Lillias. *Irish Weaving.* Dundalgan Press Dundalk, 1989

- Shaw-Smith, David. *Ireland's Traditional Crafts.* Thames and Hudson Ltd. London, 1984